N C T
RELOAD
DREAM

NCT
RELOAD
DREAM

RELOAD

NCT DREAM   RIDIN' & ROLLIN'

RENJUN

JENO

HAECHAN

 NCT DREAM RELOAD

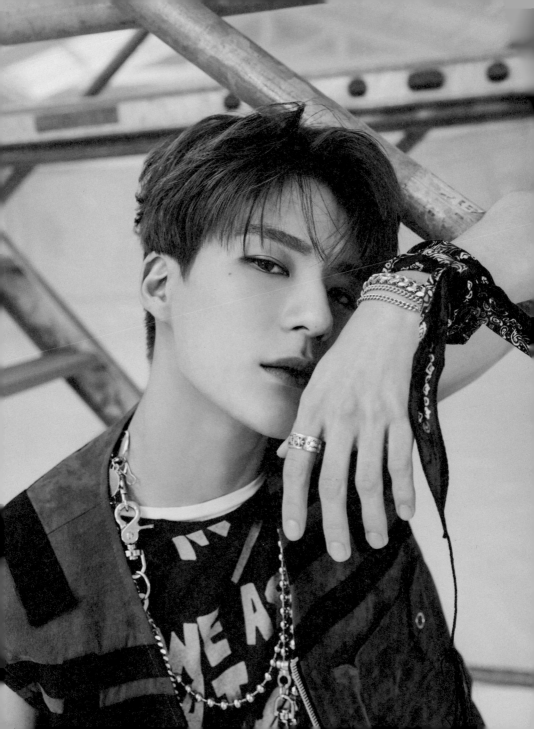

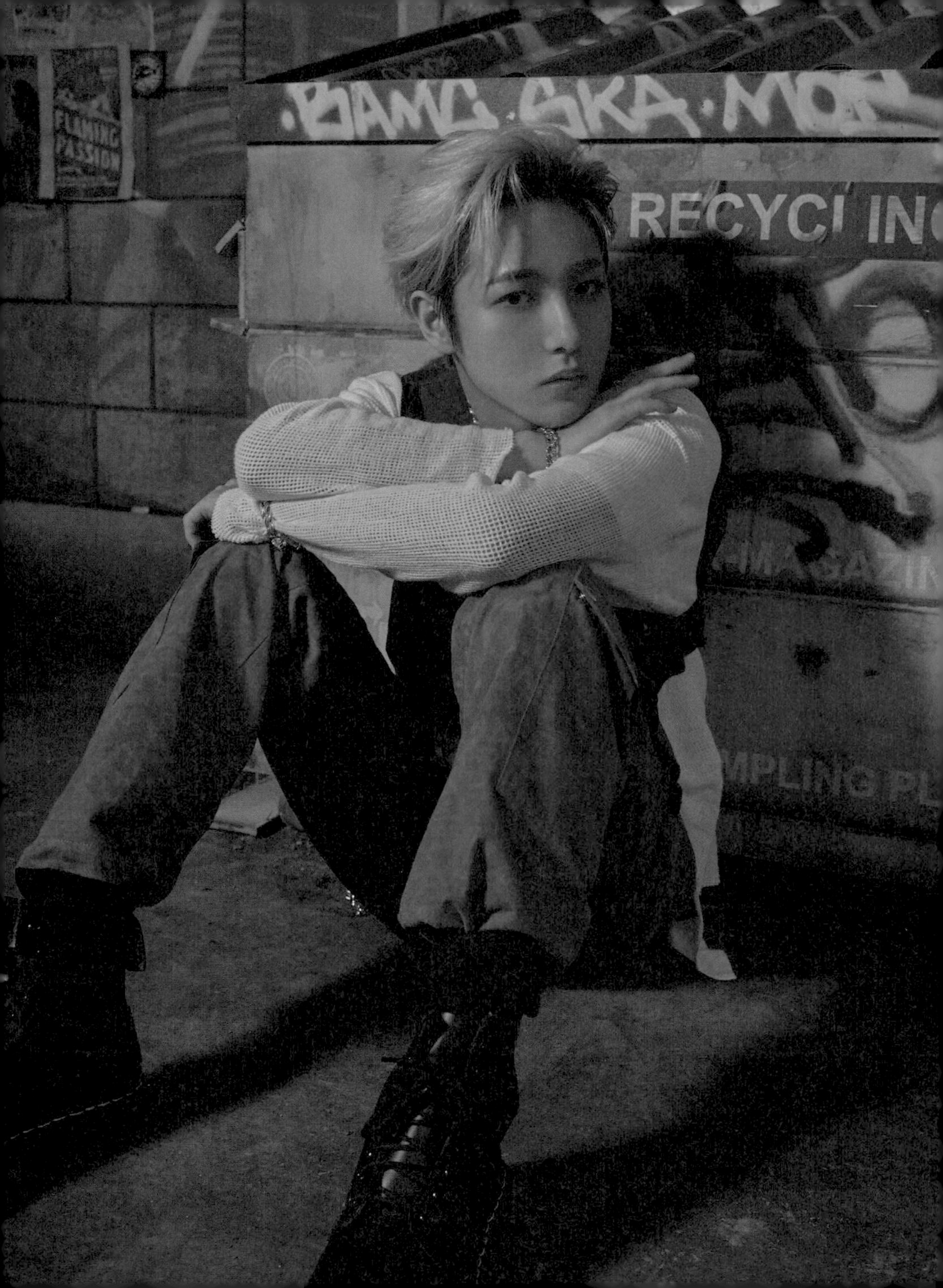
FLAMING PASSION
RECYCLING

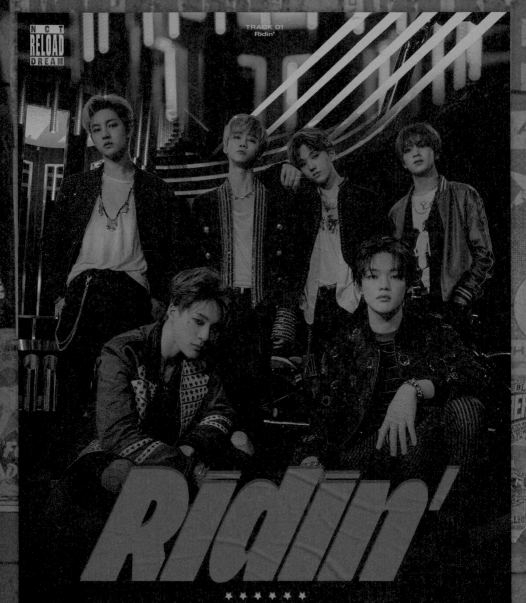

Ridin'

★ ★ ★ ★ ★ ★ ★

Korean Lyrics by 장정원(JamFactory), Rick Bridges(X&)
Composed by Moonshine, Maurice Moore, Jeremy "Tay" Jasper, Adrian McKinnon, Darius Martin, Hautboi Rich
Arranged by Moonshine
Additional Top Line & Vocal Additional Arranged by YOO, YOUNG JIN

*거리 위 텅 빈 듯한 이 느낌 열기로 가득 채워 Reloading 경계를 Break break out 어디든지 겨눠 봐 이젠 우리가 방아쇠 당겨 잘 봐 We're back No more brakes 모두 다 Sit back 이젠 마주해 날 향한 Scream 오랜 기다림의 끝에 불을 붙여 시동 거는 순간 It's game over ya Talk talk 어딜 가도 talk talk 내 얘기로 다들 떠들썩해 찢어지는 듯한 마찰음 위로 난 선을 넘어서 시간을 자유롭게 더 뜨겁게 이 순간을 달궈 Burn up the road 날 넘어설 그때까지 *REPEAT **Ridin' & Rollin' oh baby Reloading Ridin' & Rollin' oh baby Reloading 지금 우린 Running Reloading oh yea 새롭게 날 채워 다시 Whip fast 거침없이 핸들 더 꺾어 붕 뜨는 몸은 마치 Like a roller coaster 터질 듯 엑셀을 밟아봐 We outta control ya ya We won't stop the racing till it's over ya Talk talk 어떤 말도 talk talk 이 순간 속 우릴 설명 못 해 가장 눈부신 이 속도에 올라타 모두 놀랄 그 장면 속 우릴 향해 몇 번이고 한껼 뛰어넘어 Burn up the road 다시 내일이 올 때까지 ***심장 속 터질 듯한 Energy 끝까지 나를 던져 Reloading 기록은 Break break out 매번 갈아치워 가 이젠 세상에 우릴 쏴 올려 잘 봐 **REPEAT 눈 앞에 펼쳐진 세상을 봐 숨써왔던 Story 더는 꿈이 아냐 새롭게 뜬 태양을 마주 봐 Flying down the road (Let's roll) 도로 위로 가득한 붉은 불빛들은 날 멈춰 있으라지만 Woah woah woah woah 더는 같은 길을 향해 가지 않아 이젠 Switch my lane 나만의 새로운 길을 만들어 벗어나 Rush hour ***REPEAT **REPEAT

★ ★ ★ ★ ★ ★ ★

Vocal directed by DEEZ **Background vocals by** YOO, YOUNG JIN, 변장문, NCT 해찬 **Recorded by** 강은지 @ SM SSAM Studio / 권유진 @ doobdoob Studio **Digital Editing by** 장우영 @ doobdoob Studio **Engineered for mix by** 노민지 @ SM Yellow Tail Studio **Mixed by** 정의석 @ SM Blue Cup Studio

Original Title: Ridin' & Rollin' **Original Writers:** Jonatan Gusmark / Ludvig Evers / Rick Heymann / Jeremy D Jasper / Adrian McKinnon / Julien Maurice Moore / Darius Martin **Original Publishers:** EKKO Music Rights Europe (powered by CTGA) / EKKO Music Rights (powered by CTGA) / WC Music Corp. / AMM7 / STXRY Sound / Warner Chappell Music Canada Ltd. / Copyright Control **Sub-Publishers:** EKKO Music Rights (powered by CTGA) / Warner Chappell Music Korea Inc.

QUIETDOWN

RENJUN JENO HAECHAN JAEMIN CHENLE JISUNG

Quiet Down

✦ ✦ ✦ ✦ ✦ ✦

Korean Lyrics by 장한빛(JamFactory)
Composed by Timothy "BOS" Bullock, Jeremy "Tay" Jasper, SAARA, Jordain Johnson, Zachary Chicoine
Arranged by Timothy "BOS" Bullock

Yea ooh 한 번쯤은 스친 것 같아 기억은 나지 않는데 그렇다니 그런가 보네 그런가 봐 딱 한 번 지나친 Backbiter (It's like a cash) 새로울 거 없이 지루해 (C'mon) 너를 겨눠 Worry 'bout me 신경 안 써 여전히 대꾸는 없어 What you speak 잘 알잖아 넌 누굴 믿을지 *번져가는 소문 Talk to you 나를 믿는다면 Need to mute 떠들어봐 어디 Fake News Turn that shh down for quiet new dawn **어둠이 걷혀 눈을 떠봐 진실을 마주해 넌 이제 Quiet down Quiet down Quiet down 떠도는 저 거짓말 다 사라져 Quiet down 늘 타깃을 잡아 꽉 물고 늘어져 (Gotta bite) 사실은 관심도 없어 (You know) 네가 날 믿을 때 I don't hesitate 아무리 말해도 떠보고 흔들어 확인받고 싶어해 keep it keep or keep it doubt 딱 한 번 말할게 Don't worry 달라질 건 없어 알잖아 Question me question you 결국에 넌 마주해 Your self 좀 더 편하게 널 내려놔야 해 떠들어 대는 말 Don't react Just live live *REPEAT **REPEAT Just quiet down you say too much 증명할 것은 단 하나도 없어 알잖아 눈빛에 비친 너를 봐 나의 모든 방향은 너 하나를 가리켜 흐르는 시간 속에 유일한 진실 그림자처럼 결국 뒤처질 말들 Just quiet down and chillin' out 기억해 **REPEAT **REPEAT Quiet down oh

✦ ✦ ✦ ✦ ✦ ✦

Vocal directed by DEEZ Background vocals by NCT 해찬 Recorded by 정의석 @ SM Blue Cup Studio Digital Editing by 장우영 @ doobdoob Studio
Engineered for mix by 이지홍 @ SM LVYIN Studio Mixed by 이지홍 @ SM LVYIN Studio

Original Title: Quiet Down Original Writers: Timothy "BOS" Bullock / SAARA (Sara Forsberg) / Jeremy D Jasper / Wilston Jordain Johnson / Zachary Chicoine Original Publishers: Cuts of Reach Music. (c/o Timothy Harold Bullock) / The Passion Behind The Muzik / Sara Forsberg Music / BMG Gold Songs / WC Music Corp. / Beacon Copyrights (BMI) / OH LAWD ASIA (ASCAP) Sub-Publishers: Fujipacific Music Korea Inc. / Warner Chappell Music Korea Inc.

NCT
RELOAD
DREAM

NANA

Hanggisung

WATCH OUT !

Joon-Jo

LE LE

MY
DREAM

JenMoong

NCT DREAM

Fullsun

7DAYS

내게 말해줘

✦ ✦ ✦ ✦ ✦ ✦

Korean Lyrics by 강은정
Composed by Henrik Bryld Wolsing, Castle, 밍지션(minGtion)
Arranged by Easthigh, 밍지션(minGtion)

*7 Days a week 넌 어땠니 우린 꽤나 맞는 것 같니 느낀 대로만 나에게도 말해주면 돼 7 Days a week 늘 네 곁을 맴돌 테니 편하게 말해 언제라도 날 불러주면 달려가면 돼 아마 요즘 우리가 만난 날들 가운데 가장 바쁘게 지낸 특별한 일주일 같지 처음 날 보던 눈빛과 짓던 너의 미소가 아예 머릿속에서 떠날 생각이 없는 듯해 지금 난 난 난 딱 한 시간만 사실 내 내 내 맘은 이런데 아님 밤 밤 밤을 새도 좋아 (Want it want it yea want it) Woo yea 괜히 막 막 막 신경 쓰지 마 그냥 네 네 네 맘 가는 대로 나도 널 널 널 따라가려고 Yea *REPEAT 새삼 일주일이란 게 정말 짧은 것 같긴 해 너와 함께한 시간을 끝내기엔 아쉬운데 사실 난 아직 궁금해 너에 대한 모든 것 알아 가면 알수록 Oh 빠져들어 지금 난 난 난 딱 하루만 사실 내 내 내 맘은 이런데 아님 매 매 매일 함께 할래 (Want it want it yea want it) Woo yea 괜히 막 막 막 고민하지 마 그냥 네 네 네 맘 가는 대로 나도 널 널 널 따라가려고 Yea *REPEAT 늘 이쯤에서 끝나는 매번 머뭇거렸던 걸음이 나의 맘을 대신 표현해 혼자 앞서서 가긴 싫은 걸 So 뭘 하든 너라면 나도 같은 맘이니까 7 Days a week 서로에게 어떤 의미였었든 건지 시간따윈 더 원한다면 얼마든지 써 지금 내가 듣고 싶은 건 솔직한 네 진심일 뿐이야 느낀 대로만 나에게도 말해주면 돼 Uh yea 준비되면 Everyday Yea 원한다면 Every night Yea 너와 함께 있을 게 내게 말해 줘 Uh yea 오늘처럼 Everyday Yea 우리 둘은 Every night Yea 너와 함께 있을 게 내게 말해 줘

✦ ✦ ✦ ✦ ✦ ✦

Vocal directed by 밍지션(minGtion) **Background vocals by** 변장문, Castle **Recorded by** 노민지 @ SM Yellow Tail Studio / 홍성준 @ 개나리싸운드 **Digital Editing by** 노민지 @ SM Yellow Tail Studio **Engineered for mix by** 노민지 @ SM Yellow Tail Studio **Mixed by** 김철순 @ SM Blue Ocean Studio

Original Title: 7 Days A Week **Original Writers:** Henrik Bryld Wolsing / Castle **Original Publishers:** Henrik Wolsing pub designee / WC Music Corp. / Copyright Control **Sub-Publisher:** Warner Chappell Music Korea Inc.

NCT
RELOAD
DREAM

RENJUN / JENO
HAECHAN / JAEMIN
CHENLE / JISUNG

LOVE
AGAIN

사랑은 또다시

★ ★ ★ ★ ★ ★

Korean Lyrics by 신진혜(JamFactory), 정물화(JamFactory)
Composed by Mike Daley, Mitchell Owens, Jeff Lewis, Micky Blue
Arranged by Mike Daley, Mitchell Owens

큰일이 난 것 같아 (This time) 원래 이러는 거야? 말도 안 되는 거잖아 이러다가 난 다시 빠질 거야 똑같지는 않지만 (Every time) 불안한 건 사실이야 (Baby give me what you got) 왜 이러면서 네게 끌리는 걸까 어려워 좀 아직 그랬던 내가 (Hey I met you there) 너를 본 순간 (Okay now show me the way) 흔들리는 건 왤까 (Give it up or don't give it up) 겁이 나지만 네가 좋아 난 네가 하는 말 이젠 조금 알 것 같지 스쳐 가듯 뱉리지만 (속에 숨은 뜻) 눈치도 없던 그때의 난 모를 눈빛 너도 내가 궁금한 것 같아 (Let's go) *기억들이 삭제됐나 아팠던 게 기억도 안 나 Baby 너의 두 눈을 보면 예상한 적 없었던 이 날 다시 우연처럼 나타나 Baby 너의 두 눈을 보면 **Keep it on the low Keep it on the low (alright) Keep it on the low 또 이런 일이 일어날 수도 있었다는 걸 나는 됐어 안 어울려 Bad boy 굳이 애써 널 이길 생각 없어 난 너라는 미로 이미 다녀간 나 그런데 대체 왜 또 못 찾을까 출구가 없어 너에게 취하는 건 알딸딸한 기분과는 달라 몸이 가벼워 난 머리부터 발끝까지 설렘으로 샤워한 듯한 이 느낌 이럴 때 네가 뭐라 할지 알 것 같지 전부는 아니지만 (Falling in love tonight) 맘만 앞섰던 그때의 난 모를 손짓 그 의미를 이제는 알아 난 (Let's go) *REPEAT ***잠시 네가 곁에 없던 짧은 그 시간 필요했던 거야 이 결말을 위해 다 다시 처음으로 되돌아가 말해 난 Sing it Hey my first and last ***REPEAT *REPEAT 나도 이런 내가 너무 놀라워 하얀 백지장처럼 모두 지워져 Delete 두 눈을 보면 리모컨을 갖고서 누른 것처럼 그런 웃음 하나로 모든 걸 지워 Delete 두 눈을 보면 **REPEAT

★ ★ ★ ★ ★ ★

Vocal directed by 변장문 Background vocals by 변장문 Recorded by 민성수 @ doobdoob Studio / 정호진 @ sound POOL studios Digital Editing by 강은지 @ SM SSAM Studio Engineered for mix by 이민규 @ SM Big Shot Studio Mixed by 남궁진 @ SM Concert Hall Studio

Original Title: On the Low Original Writers: Mike Daley / Mitchell Owens / Jeff Lewis / Micky Blue Original Publishers: Ritchie Court (ASCAP) / EKKO Music Rights (powered by CTGA) / Mavrick Publishing c/o Downtown Music Publishing LLC / One In Song Music LLC Administered by Songs of Kobalt Music Publishing (BMI) Sub-Publichors: EKKO Music Rights (powered by CTGA) / Music Cube, Inc.

NCT
RELOAD
DREAM

TRACK 05
너의 자리|Puzzle Piece

RENJUN / JENO / JAEMIN / JISUNG / HAECHAN / CHENLE

PUZZLE
PIECE

★ ★ ★ ★ ★ ★ ★

너의 자리

★ ★ ★ ★ ★ ★

Korean Lyrics by 황유빈, 제노, 재민
Composed & Arranged by Josh Cumbee, Andrew Allen

내가 맞춰 나가는 세상이 커져 갈수록 텅 빈 허전함을 느꼈었지만 어떤 부분인지도 이런 모양일지도 나조차 알지 못했었지만 흩어져버린 조각 맞추듯이 우리의 이야기를 맞춰가고 어딘가 비어있던 내 맘속에 자리하고 있는 Piece 난 너란 걸 그냥 한눈에 알아보았어 *You're my missing puzzle piece 드디어 맞춰진 조각나 있던 맘의 상처까지 가득 채워준 넌 어느새 내 전부가 됐어 My missing puzzle piece 내게 흠이 있단게 또 완벽하지 않단게 날 작아지게 만들었지만 어쩜 그 틈 사이에 서롤 채울 수 있게 비워져 있던 걸지도 몰라 안녕 오랜만이야 오래됐지 주머니에 넣고 다니던 이 작은 조각이 더 진하게 보이게 예쁘게 함께 해줘 널 만나서 난 더 커다란 그림을 그려 *REPEAT My missing puzzle piece 모든 걸 다 갖는 것보다 무엇 하날 절대로 잃지 않는 게 더 중요한 거란 걸 너로 인해 알게 되었어 You're my missing puzzle piece 너무나 눈부신 늘 혼자 맞춰가던 세상 속 한 장면이 돼 준 꽉 끼워진 손 뺄 수 없듯이 너를 빼곤 완성될 순 없으니 우린 서롤 잃어버리지 않길 My missing puzzle piece My missing puzzle piece

★ ★ ★ ★ ★ ★

Vocal directed by 임한별 **Background vocals by** NCT 런쥔, NCT 해찬, NCT 천러 **Recorded by** 노민지 @ SM Yellow Tail Studio / 온성윤 @ sound POOL studios **Digital Editing by** 강은지 @ SM SSAM Studio **Engineered for mix by** 이민규 @ SM Big Shot Studio **Mixed by** 이민규 @ SM Big Shot Studio

Original Title: Puzzle Pieces **Original Writers:** Josh Cumbee / Andrew Allen **Original Publishers:** BMG Gold Songs / Cumbee Publishing / Kite Kid Music / Sony/ATV Tunes LLC **Sub-Publishers:** Fujipacific Music Korea Inc. / Sony/ATV Music Publishing Korea